THE CURRICULUM of the Rudolf Steiner School

Roy Wilkinson

RSCP

The publisher is grateful for the encouragement and support of Robert Dulaney in making this new edition possible.

The name Waldorf really belongs only to the first school of its type, the one founded by Rudolf Steiner in Stuttgart, Germany for the children of the workers at the Waldorf-Astoria factory. It has since been adopted as the generic name of schools conducted according to Rudolf Steiner's recommendations. In place of Waldorf some establishments call themselves Rudolf Steiner schools. Others take a distinctive name and add Waldorf or Rudolf Steiner in some connection as a subtitle.

These notes are intended for the use of teachers, parents, and all those interested in the education of the child. They are based on the author's life-long contact with Rudolf Steiner's work, including thirty years' practical experience in the classroom.

Reprinted, 1977, 1982, 1983, 1986, 1990, 1992

Revised 2000

ISBN 0-945803-51-6

Book orders may be made through Rudolf Steiner College Bookstore. Tel. 916-961-8729, FAX 916-961-3032.

Rudolf Steiner College Press
9200 Fair Oaks Boulevard
Fair Oaks, CA 95628, U.S.A.

Table of Contents

Introduction

The task of education is to help human beings to fulfill themselves. Yet how shall this be achieved if so much within them remains untouched and undiscovered? To further the development of the human being, it is not only a question of *what* is taught, but *how* and *when*. These matters are dealt with more fully in parallel publications. The object of this booklet is to give an outline of the "what" with some indications of the other aspects.

The trend of modern education has been towards a one-sided cultivation of the intellect. Learning and the learned person have been an ideal. Manual skills, artistic achievements have been less attractive. Even in the intellectual field there has been a one-sided development so that specialists of one sort and another emerge. This is not to decry specialists but to suggest that specialization should follow the acquisition of wide and general knowledge and experience.

During the past few years this one-sideness of schooling has been recognized, and in an attempt to create a balance, the so-called "comprehensive" schools have been introduced. More subjects and a great variety of them are offered, but the pattern of learning has not changed basically.

Entrance to universities and to many professions depends on passing a number of examination subjects, and this concentration on a limited number makes its influence felt right down the school. In the formative years of childhood it would be more reasonable to be developing and learning on a broader basis, for the child is still interested in all aspects of life.

The comprehensive school offers a choice from a great variety of subjects, but the emphasis is on choice and this means specialization or the neglect of certain matters, whichever way one looks at it. By contrast, if we speak of a comprehensive education, which is what the Rudolf Steiner schools claim to give, it means a partaking of all that is offered by all the pupils. In addition, a comprehensive education means much more than a training of intellectual faculties. It means development of artistic, moral and spiritual qualities. If society is a reflection of the individual, few will argue that a new impulse must be given to individuals by individuals; i.e., to pupils by enlightened teachers. It is recognised in educational circles that one of the main problems nowadays is the social and moral education of the young adult.

While this is a view we can endorse, the real question remains, how? Scientific thinking, the way in which the natural scientist thinks, objectively and detached from the personal, has penetrated into the field of education. Knowledge and information are given in schools but without reference to the human being. Of what purpose is it to study the starry heavens or the nature of the plant if the knowledge does not touch us as humans? The human being is the center of all things. To relate all things to the human being is not to foster egoism but to teach each person his or her place in the world. If knowledge is given without reference to the person, small wonder that he or she becomes apathetic or even destructive. Nature abhors a vacuum. The lack of necessary spiritual nourishment in formative years leaves the mind a prey to slogans, half-truths, and all manner of negative influences.

Rudolf Steiner paved the way towards a new type of education by pointing repeatedly to humankind as the center of the universe. He described the human being from the spiritual-scientific point of view and explained our connections with the world and the cosmos. Education begins with the study of the human being.

The education which bears Rudolf Steiner's name, also known as Waldorf Education, is liberal and comprehensive. It claims to develop the many potentialities of the human being and must therefore, of necessity, offer a wide curriculum. It includes almost everything. It encompasses not only the usual subjects, reading, writing, mathematics, history, geography, science, etc., but it includes arts and crafts and, in later years, offers a tremendous picture of the scope of human endeavor throughout evolution.

The Rudolf Steiner schools aim at developing a harmonious, well-balanced personality. This is only possible if a wide field is covered and a demand made on the many forces of the human being. Thus intellectual, artistic and practical work are balanced. Nor is it only a question of learning. The effect of learning on character and personality is of paramount importance. A great range of subjects is covered and only a particular way of working makes this possible. Briefly this is as follows.

The Rudolf Steiner School envisages twelve classes (or grades) and a kindergarten. The classes are usually numbered one to twelve. For children between the ages of six and fourteen the main subjects are taught by one teacher. The study is made in concentrated periods, i.e., two hours of one subject daily for several weeks. "Main" subjects are English, mathematics, geography, history, and the sciences. Other subjects such as languages, gymnastics, crafts, can be taught by other teachers during the course of the day. Between the ages of fourteen and eighteen, in the so-called upper school, specialist teachers are responsible for instruction. The method of teaching is adhered to in all Rudolf Steiner schools but modifications in the subjects taught may be necessary from time to time owing to local conditions. It must also be mentioned that the curriculum suggested by Dr. Steiner is not necessarily final. It should be looked upon as a guide. Education cannot be dogmatic. It is an art and arises in the interplay between teacher and subject. The method of presenting subjects and the actual sequence of presentation accord with the development of the child's own being.

In this particular description, no attempt has been made to group the subjects as arts, sciences or humanities.

In their presentation in the Rudolf Steiner school it would be difficult to make such a distinction. With the basic idea of "wholeness" and the relationship of everything to the human being, every subject becomes an art, a science and a humanity. Thus geography will embrace not only a description of the Earth and the economic factors, but also the cultures and the spiritual development of the people who inhabit the various quarters of the Earth.

For the purpose of this outline, main lesson work is taken as one section, followed by a survey of work in other fields. It is not intended to provide a complete guide for teachers but to give information likely to be of general interest. The suggestions may be regarded as an "ideal" Steiner school curriculum, and it might be possible to carry them out in ideal conditions. In an imperfect world one can only strive towards the ideal.

The degree to which the suggestions here can be accomplished will depend on many factors: local conditions, the length of the school day and term, availability of teachers and facilities, the intelligence of the pupils. The quality of Rudolf Steiner schools, like others, will vary.

Main Lesson Work

ENGLISH AND ENGLISH LITERATURE

—For routine English, a three- or four-week period every term throughout the school, and extra practice as required.

In the first and second classes the English Main Lesson period is devoted to writing, reading and speaking.

In Class One, at the age of six or seven, a beginning is made with writing. Children, who live in an imaginative world at this age, have no immediate relationship to the abstractions which we call letters. The approach to writing is therefore gradual. Children first practise movement with the whole body, such as running straight and curved lines, circles and loops, and this develops a feeling for form with the whole organism. The same movements can be described in the air by the arm. The children can then practise drawing the forms on the blackboard or on paper with elaborations; i.e., from straight and curved lines to simple repetitive patterns and completing symmetrical forms on an upright axis where one side is given.

This is a preliminary to learning the shape of the letters. Then from the children's own paintings and drawings, indicated by the teacher, the shape of the consonants can be formed; e.g., from a picture of waves the letter W can be derived; from Valley, V. Each teacher should use his/her own faculty of invention.

The vowels can be evolved from expressions of feeling. Owing to the chaotic use of vowels in English, a good imagination is sometimes required. A, pronounced AH, can be characterised as an opening out, an expression of wonder; U, pronounced OO, is the opposite, fear.

In this way each letter acquires significance. Thus children learn something about the nature of sound, of which the letter is a representation. If we consider a certain sound and then a series of words that begin with this sound, we may be able to deduce something. Take *L*, for instance, and Love, Life, Laughter. Here is an expression of an unfolding. *B* has something of the nature of enclosing. *R* has a rolling activity. (Eurythmy, an art of movement taught in all the Rudolf Steiner schools, is a great help in this respect.)

It is also essential to teach that the letters of the alphabet have a name and different pronunciations. See the author's verses in the booklet *Miscellany*. Once the idea of reality has been conveyed there is no need to deal with every letter.

There is a certain controversy among teachers over which script to use. My own opinion is to use the Latin capitals to begin with, then adapt them to cursive, which is not difficult. **W** = 𝔚 , **V** = 𝔙 ; then proceed to the lower case in cursive writing, making up a plausible story for the change. It seems to me that the cursive has the virtue of flow and is more aesthetic.

There is also a little question about the instruments used for writing. Pens and biros (ballpoint pens) seem a little harsh. Pencils are not very durable but a solution is to use coloured pencil (stick) crayons and, at first, to allow the children to write fairly large.

By the end of the first year, children should be able to recognise all the letters and be able to copy a short piece from the blackboard—preferably something of substance rather than the classical "The cat sat on the mat.'

> The sun above us, shining bright,
> Sends to earth both warmth and light.

At this stage children should also be able to express simple thoughts or give simple descriptions in writing. These can be from what they have experienced, or they can be purely imaginative—creative writing. There should be no formal spelling practice but any natural interest can be fostered. A short sentence could be dictated.

Reading follows writing. The reason for learning to write first is that more of the whole being is engaged. Writing demands a little more physical activity. Reading is more a matter of eye and brain, and it is better for general development if this intellectual activity is somewhat deferred. Children first practise reading by reading their own writing, then reading suitable printed matter. The transition from cursive to print presents no difficulty. In some cases it may be better to defer this transition to Class Two.

Much emphasis is laid on speaking. It must be the object of every teacher to acquire a good, clear, artistic way of speaking as this conveys itself automatically to the class. But more than this, in his or her way of speaking the teacher can convey a feeling for punctuation and syntax, and for the aesthetic value of words. Telling stories is the medium.

The speech of children must also be consciously developed. This is done by encouraging them to retell stories and to recite poetry whereby attention is paid to correct enunciation, expression and pauses, which in the script would be marked by punctuation. In the course of time, oral composition is practised in connection with other subjects. It is a feature of the Rudolf Steiner schools that speech in some form or other is practised every day. Perhaps fifteen minutes every morning are devoted to recitation, either choral or individual, or both. Plays can be acted, mainly with choral speaking. Miming of stories can be attempted.

There are other beneficial results of learning to speak properly. Dr. Steiner suggests that proper formation of sentences helps to produce good behaviour. Certainly to speak properly means to breathe properly, with its good effect on health. (It is not suggested that children should adhere to any particular accent. See the author's book "Speech and Speaking in the Classroom.")

Literature is introduced by the teacher telling stories and reciting poems. Fairy stories are eminently suitable for this age as they reflect the child's state of mind and at the same time provide a fund of worldly wisdom in imaginative pictures. In due course children will be able to read about the thousand and one things that are of interest in the world but for the moment the teacher can stimulate interest by what is conveyed orally; i.e., the teacher must use his or her imagination to produce stories which call the children's attention to all sorts of natural phenomena—the seasons, the weather, plant life, animals, birds, local objects of interest. These matters become 'subjects' in later classes—geography, history, botany, zoology, etc. Of course, the teacher will have a library in which to search for material but as far as nature stories are concerned, these are often trivial or include utilitarian aspects which are not considered suitable in the context of Steiner education.

Besides English, there are naturally other lessons which will provide material for practising writing, reading and speaking.

The work done in Class Two is mainly a continuation and elaboration of that done in the previous class. Small extracts of prose or poems, prepared by the teacher and written on the blackboard, are copied, attention being paid to a clear, well-formed script and punctuation. The content will be from the literature listed below and from the children's own experience. The full stop (period) and capital letters can be explained.

Reading will be from suitable literature, as listed. Speaking will be encouraged using similar material. Simple speech exercises can be practised. Children can be encouraged to describe their own experiences orally. Literature: legends, fables, folklore, nature stories as in Class One. Stories of the saints. Poems.

In Class Three the activities of writing, reading and speaking are continued to achieve greater perfection. Dr. Steiner suggests that instruction in writing business and formal letters should be given at this age, nine to ten.

At the age of nine, when children in their natural development begin to take more interest in the outer world, formal grammar is introduced. Grammar is something which has grown out of the human being and should not be thought of as something superimposed on the language. Parts of speech are the first things taught and, of these, verbs, nouns, and adjectives are of paramount importance. They should be taught in that order. As a background to the teaching—not necessarily to be conveyed to the pupil, the teacher might reflect on the origin of the parts of speech: verb, noun, adjective. In the verb is activity; in the noun, objectivity; in the adjective, subjectivity. We have a manifestation of the threefold nature of man: willing, thinking, feeling.

It is possible at this age to show the different parts of a sentence, at least the main and subordinate clauses, but children should not yet be required to analyse.

Other grammatical matters for this age are: types of nouns, gender, plurals; in punctuation: question and exclamation marks, commas. It is the author's view that from now onwards, there should be some routine spelling practice. As a general principle, no grammar books are put before the child at this age. The teacher has to be productive, and grammar and syntax are taught from examples which the teacher or the children themselves produce.

Apart from understanding grammar in its utilitarian, conventional aspect, the learning of it has a more subtle effect on the child. It brings about an awakening, a development of the forces of consciousness. In the first place the child learns to speak without any knowledge of grammar, but to become conscious of the laws means a step in evolution.

Oral work is continued, and both oral and written work can be based on topics studied in other main lessons.

Reading can be practised in unison and then singly and children should be encouraged to read intelligently, that is, to pay attention to commas, full stops, question marks, etc.

Literature. It should be mentioned that one of the main periods in this class is concerned with practical work—farming, gardening, housebuilding. Books and poems on these subjects will therefore be of interest. The special material for this class, a spiritual food, is the Old Testament stories.

In Class Four children continue to write their own accounts of stories and experiences. (In my own teaching I corrected these as far as the English was concerned and let them rewrite a corrected version.) They can copy special texts or poems from the blackboard and practise good handwriting. An ink pen or biro (ballpoint) can now be used.

At this age, ten, when a greater feeling for time develops, the tenses can be learned and studied in a more intensive way. At the same time the child will show a greater understanding for the parts of speech. Further approach can be made towards the study of the structure of sentences and grouping of words, i.e., simple, compound and complex sentences; phrases and clauses.

There are differing opinions among teachers about the use of textbooks. Ideally, it might be said that if a teacher can produce everything him- or herself in sufficient variety and quantity, the teaching will be that much more alive and stimulating. Practically, there is so much to practise that the necessary standards can scarcely be achieved without resorting to some established system.

In the abundance of interesting things to do and learn, spelling can easily be overlooked. One might wish that routine practice were not necessary but our chaotic English orthography demands it. Words thus learnt can be incorporated in a piece of dictation.

The use of the dictionary should be taught.

Class readers may be used but pupils should be encouraged to read independently, preferably well-written books with substance; also books relating to main lesson work.

Suitable speech exercises can be practised; recitation of poetry continued, especially alliterations which speak to the growing will element. Verbal descriptions can be encouraged and plays produced with individual roles.

Literature. One main lesson of this period is entitled "Human Beings and Animals." Another is "Home Surroundings" which is an elementary study of the immediate environment. Books relative to these themes may support the lessons. The rumbustious Norse stories accord with chronological development.

In Class Five the concepts of writing, reading and speaking can scarcely be considered as separate subjects any longer. They merge together in the study of English. Although new material is being introduced, it must be emphasised that continual practice is necessary in what has already been acquired, including the art of speaking.

Spelling still presents difficulties to some pupils and often needs particular attention. Every child should learn to write clearly and legibly and practice may also be necessary, but better handwriting may be achieved by practising form and free geometrical drawing than by actual writing.

Several times in his lectures, Dr. Steiner mentions business letters. The point at issue is that children should learn to express themselves clearly and concisely. This also applies to the making of summaries and reports.

In this class, and at the age of eleven, there is a greater separation in the child's mind between the self and the world, and hence this is the right time to learn of direct and indirect speech. The child can now grasp the concept of "classification" and this can be applied to grammatical studies: i.e., classification of nouns, pronouns, verbs; the use of prefixes and suffixes; comparison of adjectives and adverbs; active and passive forms of the verb.

In writing, this is a transitional period. Up to now, what children have written must have been based, in the main, on what has been explained or read. The child has needed a guiding line. Now a change can be made to the individual arrangement of ideas, i.e., free composition.

All punctuation should now be practiced.

Literature. Main lesson subjects include Ancient Civilizations (mythologies), India, Persia, Egypt, possibly Greece; Plant Study, Geography (study of the extended locality). Suitable literature in these subjects may now be studied but the field is wide open; e.g., Biographies, the Gospels, Novels, Poetry.

Class Six. Further practice in all aspects is required and as English is the medium of instruction, the process will be continuous. Judicious use of textbooks is possible.

With regard to new material in the specific English lessons, further study can be made of the more remote aspects of verbs, transitive and intransitive, infinitive forms, participles, verbal nouns. Modal verbs should be explained. We can continue to deal with subject, object, predicate, moods—indicative, imperative, subjunctive. A few happy periods can be spent dealing with antonyms, synonyms and homonyms.

With the developing intellectual faculty, formal composition can now be expected, including the different types—imaginative, expository, descriptive. There should be no more copying from the blackboard except on special occasions. The teacher can dictate notes and the pupils write them up in essay form.

At the age of twelve an aesthetic feeling for language can be consciously cultivated. This means studying verse forms, rhythms and metre of poetry; also the differing qualities of epic, lyric and dramatic poems. A study is made of the figures of speech, and some sort of feeling for the sound of language is fostered as well as the styles of writing.

Literature. A special main lesson period is concerned with Roman and Medieval history and themes relative to this suggest themselves. Further material would be Tales of Chivalry, King Arthur stories, Biographies, Novels, Poetry.

Upper School. Ages fifteen to eighteen.

In the upper school, ages fifteen to eighteen, the scope is only limited by the capacity of the pupils, and maybe the capability of the teacher. The horizon is vast and much depends on the discretion of the individual teacher who must always bear in mind the educational factor. Knowledge is one thing, but the effect of that knowledge is another. The following can be considered as suggestions.

At the age of puberty, with a dawning awareness of the riddles of existence, it is of therapeutic value to study Shakespeare. Here one not only meets problems but the soul is also exercised in experiencing the contrasts between comedy and tragedy. Similar features are found in Dickens. The history of drama can be studied from its religious origins. Production of plays, in addition to their artistic value, provide an exercise in co-operation..

At about the age of sixteen, a study is made of poetry as an art. All possible factors are studied as pupils can be encouraged to try their hand (or should it be brain and heart?) in composing poems. Acquaintance is made with great works of past ages: the Gilgamesh Epos, the Eddas, Kalevala, Nibelungenlied, Odyssey, the Old Testament as literature, Medieval Romance, Chaucer.

This is continued in the next class by studying the lives and works of poets and writers of the Age of Reason and Enlightenment. Grail legends can be studied and particularly the story of Parzival. Dante and Goethe should find a mention.

Towards the end of school life, age eighteen, a special study is made of modern literature illustrating issues of the present age.

Studying literature means studying (and understanding, we hope) the evolution of humanity, i.e., ourselves. Thus the development of literature is studied with this point of view in mind. For example, the story of Odysseus is an account of the human being's search for his or her own soul. Inspiration is given by Athena who represents the power of thought. The story of Parzival shows how, through ignorance, suffering and doubt, wisdom and the ability to help others is acquired. (The teacher, naturally, has to be a genius to cope with, and select from, the wealth of material available.) At the same time it is essential for the adolescents to use their own faculties of perception and judgement, and themes are given to them with indications as to how they should be worked out. An example would be to contrast the *Eumenides* of Aeschylus with Shakespeare's *Macbeth,* and to note the change in human experience. In Greek times the human being felt himself directed by the gods; in modern times the self-dependent ego consciousness has evolved. These matters can be deduced from the study of literature.

All through the school, poetry plays a part. The aim is to let pupils learn good poetry, which, in itself, forms a basis for appreciation of good English, particularly its artistic aspect. Poems, therefore, are chosen from the best poets—Shelley, Shakespeare, Milton, Byron, Longfellow, Wordsworth—also passages from the Bible.

MATHEMATICS

—One period of three or four weeks every term, and continual practice as required.

The mathematics curriculum is by far the most difficult to devise. Discrepancy in ability shows itself in this subject more than any other. Pupils appear to fall roughly into three categories: those who understand at the first explanation; those who understand after a time with a little perseverance; those who do not understand and apparently never will. Yet the teacher has to cater for all the pupils, and has also to bear in mind that certain mathematical processes constitute the right pedagogical food for certain ages and that therefore the slow learners must be encouraged to try to digest it. At the same time the latter must also be doing work with which they can cope. It is a dilemma which usually has to be solved by working in groups.

What was said in the introduction about an "ideal" curriculum has particular application here.

All branches of mathematics are taught at the Rudolf Steiner schools. The first lessons in arithmetic, to children aged six, are introduced in story form, and number work is helped through rhythmic movement—running, clapping and jumping. Numbers are explained in a qualitative as well as a quantitative sense, and the first approach is by proceeding from the whole to the parts. First there is unity, and then dispersal. There is a moral quality in this. To add is to collect to oneself and become greedy. To divide or subtract from a whole and share it is to foster generosity. In the first year the simple arithmetical processes are introduced and the four rules learned more or less together.

The writing of numbers, the figures, is taught, preferably connecting something real with the cipher as in the case of learning the written characters of the alphabet.

Simple mental sums are practised.

Children of this age are learning to write, but as a preliminary they are running straight lines and curves, circles and figure eights. In eurythmy they are practising moving in triangles, squares, spirals and even pentagrams. There is therefore here a basis for geometry as well.

A beginning can be made in this class with freehand drawing of geometrical figures.

In the second year the tables are learned. They are learned in all sorts of different ways, i.e., 12 = 3 x 4, 3 x 4 = 12, 4 x 3 = 12, 12 ÷ 3 = 4, etc. A "magic square" can be made.

The system of units, tens and hundreds is taught and the form of the sum for simple addition, subtraction, multiplication and division.

The drawing of geometrical forms can be continued and extended; a useful exercise is to complete a symmetrical pattern where one half has already been given.

Bearing in mind that the teaching must be in tune with growth, the important thing in Class Three (age nine) is to learn the weights and measures. (It is a matter of regret that some of our English weights and measures, so interesting historically, have been abandoned.) In the main lesson, the subjects of farming and housebuilding are being taken, and it is relatively easy to include work with weights and measures in their practical application. At the same time and by the same token, mathematical exercises in other respects are possible, as for instance, modeling or drawing houses, barns, haystacks. These can lead to the more abstract shapes of cubes, pyramids, cones, prisms.

The use of the ruler can be introduced and attempts made to draw simple shapes accurately.

Most children can tell the time nowadays by the age of nine, but this would be a good point at which to study the clock, and at the same time learn something of number systems; i.e., the hours of the day, the days of the week and of the year.

As the unity of the world begins to disappear in the child's mind and various subjects establish themselves in their own right (history, geography) so the time comes when the whole can be divided into parts. Thus at the age of ten, the moment has come to learn about fractions and all that goes along with them. To deal with both vulgar and decimal fractions is quite a long process and teachers should not let themselves become disheartened if they are not immediately understood.

What might be called "experimental geometry" can now be practised. A child of ten, in possession of a ruler, compasses and a little guidance, will soon discover a good many geometrical truths.

Although new work is being introduced, it is essential not to lose sight of what has already been taught, and continual practice is necessary in processes already learned.

In Class Five, or Six in some cases, children can begin to come to grips with conceptual matters, i.e., they can begin to learn practical geometrical constructions—bisecting angles, drawing perpendiculars and the circumcircle of a triangle. It is possible to appreciate visually the Theorem of Pythagoras.

In connection with the main lesson work on plants, there is a good opportunity to study geometrical harmony, particularly configurations based on the pentagram and hexagram.

The Rule of Three is studied (unitary method) and there should still be a good deal of mental arithmetic.

Approaching the age of twelve and with a greater understanding of the material world, it is fairly obvious around what the mathematical instruction should center—money. All aspects can be studied: percentage, discount, profit and loss, currency exchange, perhaps even devaluation.

The developing capacity of conceptual thinking now allows, perhaps demands, the introduction of geometry as, for instance, theorems dealing with the angles of a polygon, of a triangle, conditions under which triangles are congruent.

Formulae will have been used in calculating percentages and this forms a bridge to algebra, which is introduced in Class Seven (age thirteen).

A great deal of work based on the Theorem of Pythagoras can be done here, as applied to engineering structures and navigation. Other work is the calculation of areas, learning to find square roots and the use of negative numbers.

In the final class of the lower school there should be much revision and extension of work already introduced. It is essential that before entering the upper school, pupils are sufficiently grounded in the fundamentals of mathematics.

New work should be in financial matters—balance sheets, mortgages, hire-purchase arrangements; also in calculating volumes and making graphs. The theorems of Euclid can now be studied, learned, and pupils should be set geometrical problems based on them.

It is worth repeating that the age of fourteen is a great staging post in human development. With the onset of puberty the physical body changes and so do the mind and intellect. The faculties of perception and judgement come to the fore. The thinking becomes sharper and more critical. The education is designed to meet these growing faculties and to further them. At the same time, practical aspects must be borne in mind as well as "whole" development.

Mathematics offers enormous scope. For practical purposes it is necessary to be able to move quickly and consciously in the world of number and form (geometry) and to be able to order one's thoughts. For the mind or soul, it is good to realize and experience that there is a vast choice of things to be done and an even vaster choice of ways of carrying them out. It is salutary to realize and experience that problems can only be solved after mastering discipline in ideas, and to appreciate also that the aspect of an object can change with the viewpoint, but that essentials remain. Thus, among the studies in Class Nine (age fifteen) will be permutations and combinations, algebraical multiplication, quadratic equations, fractional and negative indices, projective geometry.

This sort of work is continued into Class Ten and trigonometry added. This has a very practical application in navigation, surveying, astronomy and structural mensuration. Logarithms are introduced here.

Remembering the expanding consciousness of the adolescent and the teacher's desire to present the world as a whole, some study should be made in this year, perhaps on the Platonic saying "God geometrizes." In other words, number, and number combinations, are to be found everywhere—in the universe, in the human being, in nature, in music.

Some indications of the laws of perspective can be given here if these have not been covered in art lessons.

Trigonometry is continued in Classes Eleven and Twelve, and in the latter also projective geometry, dealing with elements and axioms of three-dimensional space and practical applications in architecture. Where possible, an introduction is given to calculus.

All mathematical disciplines are studied as far as required for university entrance. A history of the development of mathematics through the ages is given.

Calculators. Mathematics develops the mind. Calculators do not. It is therefore recommended that their use be deferred to the upper school when basic mathematical processes should have been mastered.

Note: It must be pointed out that most of the above indications are concerned with the introduction of new work to accord with the pupil's age. Revision and continual practice may be necessary in the other endless fields of mathematics.

HISTORY

—One period of three or four weeks every year from Class Six to Class Twelve. Indian, Persian, Egyptian, Greek mythology in one or two periods of three to four weeks in Class Five, then history proper.

History is the story of humanity. Single dates and events may be outstanding, but to learn these is of less importance than to grasp the idea of human development as a whole. Every person is a part of history and the child should be brought to realize that he or she is also concerned in it. It must be made clear that if we talk about the achievements of the Greeks or the Romans, these were not isolated and independent events on the stage of history, but that our present development and ideas are intimately connected with them, as indeed with all the past. The present is the result of the past, and the future will be the result of the present. There can be no divisions.

The sense of time is also important for children. They are taking part in certain events: their parents experienced others, and their grandparents yet others. In a hundred years there are three generations, so seven generations would take us back to George Washington, fifteen to Columbus, and sixty to the time of Christ. Our ancestors experienced these events. If children can establish a personal relationship with historical figures and happenings, history is of interest and of some educational value.

As with all teaching, the teacher is the vital factor. In teaching history, teachers have to be able to digest the facts and reproduce in descriptions the personalities of history and events, so that they live in their re-creation in the mind's eye of the pupil.

In England, history begins at a certain date according to the school one has attended. It may be with Julius Caesar landing in Britain in 55 B.C. or with William the Conqueror in 1066 A.D. Each country will have its own specifically important date. Rudolf Steiner education takes a somewhat broader view than this and deals with world history from ancient times. As a preliminary to history teaching as well as to other subjects, the children of Class Four are given a period known as "Knowledge of Home Surroundings." This includes an historical survey of the immediate neighborhood. In Class Five, descriptions are given of the ancient cultures and the mentality of the peoples. Historical records of the ancient peoples do not exist, but one can infer a great deal from the mythologies.

Great periods of culture occur approximately every 2,000 years. The most ancient from which stories have come down is the civilization of Ancient India, about 7,000 B.C. This was followed by Ancient Persia, the Egyptian-Chaldean-Assyrian epoch and then the Greco-Roman one. Of these ancient civilizations much can be told from the traditional stories, leading gradually to a more definite history. Thus by Class six, the history of the Greeks and Romans is taught, and the influence of this epoch in the following centuries.

It should always be remembered that what is taught is in accordance with the child's growth. In Class Six, at the age of twelve, children stand quite firmly on the earth.

They have more interest in material things and an understanding for causality. At the same time they are more aware of themselves as individuals, so Roman history accords with their own development.

The scope of history is so wide that it is impossible to deal with everything in detail, but certain matters are important, viz., (at this age) the establishment of the Roman Empire, the meeting of Jewish, Greek and Roman civilization in Palestine, the breakdown of the Empire, the Holy Roman Empire under Charlemagne, the Middle Ages and the Crusades.

The Reformation and the Renaissance are turning points and must be accorded an important place.

With an awakening mind and a widening outlook, the next period is also momentous for adolescents. It is the Age of Discovery and the rise of natural science. It is important to note the change in astronomical thought and the practical results of the inventive mind.

The Industrial Age is the next chapter (Class Eight) and the effects of inventions on social life. The Thirty Years' War and the French Revolution need to be dealt with.

In the first class of the upper school, Class Nine, the attempt should be made to bring the historical survey up to date. The themes include the birth of the European nations and the connection with America; Imperialism and Colonisation; the First World War and its aftermath; the Treaty of Versailles; the Russian Revolution and Communism; Fascism in Germany and Italy; events in the Middle and Far East; the Second World War; freedom movements in Africa and India. A glance should be made at what is happening in all other parts of the world.

The teacher is striving to give a picture of world events. National history is taught within the framework of world history.

In the remaining classes the aim is to make a survey over the whole field of history, a recapitulation which will show how the consciousness of the human being has expanded. The Ancient Civilisations will be reconsidered in this light and other events re-assessed in the light of newfound faculties of observation and judgement: Greece, Rome and its Empire, the Migrations, development of Christianity, Norman Conquest, feudalism, Islam, the emergence of cities, Capitalism, Trade Unions. Questions might be posed as to the future. All these studies should be supported by reference to biographies.

When time allows, there are endless side studies which may be of interest: e.g., monastic life, the Cathars, origin and development of writing. These could be given as individual projects. Biographies also lend themselves to this type of work.

GEOGRAPHY

—One period of three or four weeks every year from Class Five onwards.

Mention was already made of the study of home surroundings given to Steiner school children at the age of ten. In this study are contained the beginnings of geography. The children have been made familiar with the geographical features of their immediate environment.

Whereas it can be said of history that it leads to an understanding of the inner nature of human beings, geography leads into the wide spaces and teaches them about the world as their workplace. Giving knowledge of the outer world develops a feeling of separation and thus an inner consolidation.

As with all other subjects of the Rudolf Steiner school curriculum, geography is dealt with comprehensively, that is to say, it is correlated with other subjects, such as geology, botany, zoology, history and human evolution.

A start is made at the age of eleven by transferring what has been studied under "Home Surroundings" into a map. Thus what has been experienced directly is transformed into a sort of abstract. Now the horizon is widened a little, and rivers, mountains and other features of the landscape are introduced into the map. It is usual to make pictorial maps with the forests represented by little drawings of trees, the mountains drawn somewhat to shape, and historical features like castles or cathedrals actually drawn on a small scale.

The child's outlook at this age is an expanding one and geography supports this. Having studied the vicinity one extends in all directions. In England, of course, one soon reaches the sea and England can be dealt with as a compact unit. Then one proceeds in widening circles until the whole earth is encompassed. In this way a connecting link is fostered. Otherwise a teacher may give, let us say, excellent lessons on Brazil, but Brazil remains remote and unconnected with the child's own being. The pictorial representations should be accompanied by traveller's descriptions. If the teacher is a much-travelled person, so much the better; he or she will then speak from experience.

During the ages of ten, eleven and twelve, geography is studied in ever-widening circles as described, supported by descriptions and tales on the part of the teacher and pictorial images by the children. In a general sense the material given up to the age of twelve should deal with the gifts of the Earth; from twelve onwards, the uses the human being makes of the gifts and their influences upon him. At this age, too, something of climatology should be added and something about the Earth in its cosmic setting—Astronomy.

In the next year special studies are made of economic conditions, industry, communications and of the spiritual outlook of the various peoples, the different civilisations. At some point here the political aspects are mentioned to make children aware of such matters, but not to enter into controversies.

In the upper school, between the ages of fourteen and eighteen, one can enter into questions of causality and interrelationships with regard to economy, communications, culture. There is revision and extension into the fields of geology, map projections and surveying. In Class Nine a special study is made of rocks and the associated scenery, also the main mountain formations of the Earth.

A theme for Class Ten might centre round the distribution of water and currents in the oceans. The distribution of resources is another theme. Indeed at this age pupils should take a look at the Earth as a whole, noting contrasts geographically between east and west but also realising that there is a common humanity.

At the present time of global warming and threatening catastrophes, it would be appropriate to devote further time to studying climate and factors influencing climate: release of noxious gases into the air, destruction of forests, monoculture and agribusiness.

Further, economic aspects should be considered: trade and trade agreements, European Common Market and other regional agreements, European Common Agricultural Policy, exploitation of resources and of fellow human beings.

Linked with Geography could be a study of mineralogy and crystalography, also of metals and their effects on human beings. A project considering the process of limestone and its significance in earth and human beings would be appropriate.

These studies can be continued into the next classes but there should also be a final review of the Earth as a whole, in connection with paleontology and ethnography.

NATURE STUDY AND SCIENCE

—Stories in Classes One through Three as convenient.
One or two periods of three or four weeks every year further.

Under this composite title are included a number of subjects quite special to Rudolf Steiner schools which are difficult to classify. "Nature Study and Science" is here used as a comprehensive term to express knowledge of the world.

Nature study is to connect children with their surroundings, to learn to understand them and thus find their own position in the world. In the early years the child does not feel separated from the world and nature study is therefore a matter of artistic appreciation and not scientific understanding. Up to the age of nine it is a matter of stories about familiar things which appeal to the imagination and feelings, or talks on objects in the immediate surroundings, but not in a pedantic way. To the child, everything is living. With the adult intellect we destroy life and dissect, but the child endows inanimate objects with life and feeling. Thus one speaks to the child about familiar objects as if they held converse with one another. All things are living beings. The wind talks to the trees and the sun to the flowers and in the conversations the objects can be characterized. Nature can be made to live more vividly by speaking about elemental beings.

At the age of nine, and with a step down onto the earth, "Farming and Gardening" is an important study. Very much can be introduced here in the way of nature study and general knowledge although the basic object now is to describe practical work. The teacher now has the opportunity of speaking about soil and the way it can be kept healthy. He speaks about the various crops, crop rotations, and the interplay of sun, rain and soil. He characterizes the unity and harmony in nature. Essentially, however, this period is an introduction to practical work and practical work must be described and performed where possible. This also includes a description of the gardener's and farmer's tools—on the one hand the hand tools which are used in the garden, and by contrast, their modification into farming implements when work is done on a big scale. Children should also see things in action and be taken to farms where they can watch the real work.

In this period too the various domestic animals are described, and the way in which they serve man.

A similar introduction to practical life is given under the heading of "Housebuilding," where the work of all the people concerned in building is described—the architect, bricklayer, joiner, plumber, electrician, laborer. It can also be shown that building a house is a very social project, as in some way almost the whole world takes part in it. Mining and quarrying are other practical occupations which can be studied.

At the age of ten, children are interested in their immediate surroundings. Rudolf Steiner education meets this interest by giving knowledge of everything in the locality. A start is make by a description of the origin and growth of the very place where the school is situated. What were the factors which led people to settle in this particular spot, and how has it progressed? There is thus a connection with history. But the reasons for settling are often geographical or geological, so these are further aspects. Now in this particular locality there are trees and flowers native to it and certain animals. Perhaps wind and weather provide certain characteristics. All these things are combined under a title which is "Knowledge of Home Surroundings." This forms a basis for what afterwards become the separate subjects of history, geography, botany, animal study and geology.

At this age the child stands opposite nature in a more objective way and a period is taken entitled "The Human Being and the Animal World." This is not yet Zoology, but an elementary study of the human being, and the relationship of the human being to the animal kingdom.

Each animal species presents a one-sided development which is harmonized in the human being. In a sense, the animal has achieved greater perfection, but this is also its limitation. It is more perfect in one particular direction. The human being is in this sense less perfect, but more harmonious. It will be seen that the manifold forms of the animal kingdom are unified in harmony in the human. It is a great moment for the child to experience that what is spread out in the animal world is concentrated in the human being.

After an elementary study of the human being and the animal world one progresses to the plants. Here again, it is not a question of a scientific study of the science of botany, but an appreciation of the living plant in its connections with Earth and cosmos. Descriptions, possibly poetic descriptions, should be given.

In considering the plant between heaven and Earth, one sees how the root belongs to the Earth and is of the nature of the earth. The flower is ethereal and partakes of the qualities of air and light. The green leaves form the connection and balance.

In the plant world nature expresses herself in a multitude of ways, yet it is one world which the plants manifest.

One can find the most wonderful geometrical designs in flowers, pointing almost to a mathematical concept. The connection between flowers and insects illustrates the interdependence of things in nature. The metamorphosis of the plant, that is, Goethe's idea that the plant exists and grows by a series of expansions and contractions of one basic unit, can be an educative factor for the mind.

Other points in the teaching on plants are: the vegetational regions, i.e. the effect of climate on growth and form; the stages of plant development, i.e., the sequence of growth from the simple form of the fungus through lichen, algae, moss, fern, to the flowering plant which completes its cycle from seed to seed. Some idea can be given of the Linnean orders of plants as a matter of passing interest.

In Classes Seven and Eight (ages thirteen and fourteen), perhaps a further period can be taken dealing with trees. This would deal not only with shape and growth but also with the uses of various timbers. In the same line of thought one might speak of herbs and their healing qualities.

Following quite naturally the study of plants is geology. If we take a trip across England, we can observe a great variety of geological formations, and we can also observe the connection between the Earth's crust and vegetation. In the flat, fertile vale of Evesham are the market-garden crops and the plums; on the Pennine moors, heather. In the rich fields of Buckinghamshire are the beech forests. The grass on the limestone uplands has a different hue from that on the Millstone Grit. The black earth of the Fenlands lends itself to bulb growing and grain crops. When these things have been observed, a closer acquaintance with the minerals can be made.

Thus, between Classes Four and Seven, a survey has been made of the kingdoms of nature. An elementary but artistic study of the human being comes first, then animals, something about human anatomy, physiology, facts about nutrition and the maintenance of good health.

One of the most difficult tasks in the Rudolf Steiner schools is to teach physics and chemistry, the so-called lifeless world. Concepts and ideas change rapidly. What is scientific in one century may be hocus-pocus in the next. If one has the usual natural scientific way of thinking, physics and chemistry can be taught in the usual materialistic way. If, however, one's understanding of the world and matter is colored by spiritual science, it is difficult to accept all the usual theories.

Dr. Steiner recommends that experiments be shown and then the Socratic method of questioning be adopted. The phenomena are observed and described. But children should not be entirely detached from what is happening. Their feelings should be stimulated by what they see and hear.

There is the basic fact that in Rudolf Steiner's conception of the world, the Earth and all that it contains, including human beings, have evolved from a living spiritual source. The cosmos and Earth are not dead mechanisms consisting of so many parts, but form a unity and a whole.

An effort is made in the science teaching to stimulate the whole being of the pupil; to show that there is, or has been, a creative reality in all the phenomena; to develop an understanding of all nature, to inculcate some awareness of the implications of science and not to treat it as so much factual knowledge; to stimulate creativity and imagination. In this way more of his or her being is concerned and educated than the mere intellectual forces.

The sciences of physics and chemistry are introduced in Class Six, when the children are about twelve years of age. This is the time when children develop a greater understanding of matter because they themselves are entering more into the physical world.

Again we see how teaching is structured to accord with human development. At the age of twelve, children become awkward and clumsy. This is because they are not quite happy in their body. The spirit is taking a firmer hold and entering, so to speak, the bony system.

The child's path of learning is from the artistic to the scientific. Thus acoustics is approached via music, and the relationship to the human being is shown in ear and voice. The forming principle of sound is demonstrated by the Chladne plate. The number relationships of musical intervals are shown on the Monochord.

Optics and the phenomena of color and light are approached via painting; an elementary study is made of light, of the relationships between light, dark and color, and of the complementary colors.

In practice then, the age of twelve is the time to introduce the first true physics and chemistry lessons, elementary acoustics, and optics. It is the time for the first lessons on heat—conduction, convection, radiation, contraction, expansion. This is also the time when the mind begins to expand, and hence much other material can be included such as elementary astronomy, and connections with time, moon phases, eclipses and seasons. These matters can also be dealt with in the geography lessons.

In Classes Seven and Eight (ages thirteen and fourteen) studies are continued to include magnetism, electricity, hydraulics and mechanics. As a general principle, a start should be made with examples from practical life, e.g., in mechanics the law of the lever is explained by means of the balance or some practical application of the lever.

The human being must never be left out in studying the sciences. Human beings are subject to processes of chemistry and physics. The laws of mechanics apply in their movements.

Chemistry is the branch of natural science which deals with the composition and properties of different kinds of matter, solids, liquids, gases, and their reactions on each other in various conditions. Our modern world would be unthinkable without the science of chemistry. This is first brought to the consciousness of the child in the phenomena of hard water, rust on iron, green on copper, spa waters, the breathing of plants, the nitrogen-fixers. In the human being there is the breathing and also the digestive system. Observation should be made of burning processes and the action of air on a flame. As a simple example, the teacher can strike a match and let the children observe the phenomenon. Only afterward should he or she give the explanations. The nature and use of various substances such as water, lime, sulphur, salt, should be discussed. For instance: Lime is used in agriculture. It is also used in steel processes, bleaching powders, mortar and cement. Mortar is formed by mixing slaked lime with water. After it has been exposed, it becomes a rocky substance firmly adhering to the bricks. Chemical processes in industry should be studied, and the structure of organic substances such as starch, sugar, protein and fat. Coal and its uses are very fruitful subjects of study.

These are the themes in chemistry for Classes Seven, Eight and Nine. Never should the connecting link with the human being be lost. Thus the study of the organic substances will be related to human nourishment, as was mechanics to the human structure. Eventually the student will realize that the human being contains a world within; an understanding will develop of the individual as a microcosm.

The understanding of this aspect is further fostered in the upper school, Classes Nine to Twelve, ages fourteen to eighteen, when the intellectual powers begin to work more strongly.

At puberty a twofold development is taking place in the human being. On the one hand there is physical maturity with all that it involves; on the other, there is the striving towards the ideal.

The dual nature must be catered for and this is done by studying matters appertaining to practical life; by studying the application of laws already observed, i. e., the physical principles to machines or appliances—the steam engine, internal combustion engine, diesels, jets, turbines, electric motors, telephone, radios, x-rays, television, computers, nuclear reactors and the atom bomb. Some of these subjects might lead to lively discussions. It must also be considered how inventions affect our lives and that there is a negative side to so-called progress, e.g., pollution.

On the ideal side it can be shown that the history of the development of machinery and appliances shows a mastery of the physical world. It is an illustration of the power of mind over matter. It shows that what happens in physical substance is governed by ideas. This obviously has moral implications.

In Class Nine a study of human physiology is undertaken. The main organs and their functioning form the central theme but there should be further study of acoustics in connection with the human ear. Study of optics would include photography, the microscope and the telescope.

In Class Ten the study includes the nerve-sense system, blood circulation and digestive processes. It should be pointed out that any study of physiology or anthropology is taken according to the understanding of the human being as given by Rudolf Steiner. In his conception, man is a being of body, soul and spirit, of divine origin, and it is the object of these studies to give some understanding in this light without being dogmatic.

In Class Ten, age sixteen, after the first stresses of puberty, a certain objectivity in outlook begins to develop, and the correct sort of study is that of the laws themselves—the changes which bring about the phenomena. Meteorology is a case in point. A study of botany will include a study of the soil and all influences on plant growth. If not already taken, astronomy has a place here, and its connections with life on Earth, also further studies in botany, chemistry and zoology—extended to include ecology.

The work continues through the next class to the final school year when the object should be to look at all subjects from as many points as possible, e.g. to look at the theory of color from both the Newtonian and the Goethean aspect; to look at various theories of evolution; to gain an insight into the difference between chemical processes in humans and those in nature.

At all stages studies should be interwoven with and supported by stories of the lives of inventors and pioneers.

It is a feature of the Rudolf Steiner schools that adolescents shall have first-hand acquaintance with industry. When they are about seventeen, therefore, arrangements are usually made to visit all sorts of industrial plants, factories and mines. They should learn about the origin of raw materials and their transformation. The manufacture of paper is a good example, as also the manufacture of synthetic fabrics.

In the lower school a period of farming was taken and an elementary study of animals and the human being was made. It should have been possible at some point to mention sex and the processes of reproduction and to explain the necessary facts objectively and without embarrassment. The subject could also have been introduced in other contexts and dealt with as far as necessary to satisfy the immediate moment.

In Class Nine are periods of study which can be entitled Physiology or Anthropology. They embrace the threefold aspect of the human being, the study of the main organs and their functions, the muscle system, the anatomy of the skeleton. They should also include embryology, reproduction, the sex factor, love, sexuality, social, moral and hygienic matters, health and nutrition. This might also be the place to discuss alcohol, nicotine and drugs, their uses, misuses and their effects on human beings.

Subjects Not Taken in Main Lessons

LANGUAGES

—Each language taken two or three times weekly.

Two modern foreign languages are introduced to the children of Class One. In England these are usually French and German, but in other parts of the world other languages may be chosen. It is not only a matter of becoming familiar with other tongues for practical purposes. There is another reason. There is no such thing as real translation. A word in one language expresses a particular aspect; the equivalent word in another language expresses a different one. Thus the English word *river* refers to the form of the banks, while the German *Fluss* means the flow. In learning a foreign language, therefore, one automatically widens the horizon.

As children we learn the mother tongue from our surroundings—from hearing the language spoken. This is the principle which is followed in the early school years. From the ages of six to nine, all teaching is by word of mouth. The children learn songs, poems, action songs and expressions. If the content or the words are not completely understood, it is of no great consequence. A feeling and understanding of the language is fostered on a deeper level than the intellectual. The teacher tells stories and conducts the whole of the lesson as far as possible without using the native language.

In this conversational method children become acquainted with the sound, tone, cadence and dynamics, and as the speech organs are still very flexible, it is easier for them to acquire a good accent. Language is fundamentally a spoken art. Much speaking is done, and writing is left until later.

At the age of ten, grammar is introduced, more or less parallel with the grammar teaching in the native tongue.

Every lesson should contain something imaginative and if the teacher can produce this, there is no boredom in learning. A start should be made with the verb. Tenses are learned by keeping up a rhythmic element. They are committed to memory in this way even if they are not fully understood until later. At this age also a start is made with writing, reading and general translation. Making translations is not a particularly effective way of learning. It is better to learn directly, to read and try to bring one's own thoughts to expression. In this way one learns to think in the foreign language and not to be dependent on the dual process of thinking in one language and translating as one goes along. This is, of course, not easy at the age of ten or eleven, or at any age for that matter, until one has acquired a certain facility. In the course of the school, however, the teacher can demand an increasing measure of ability and greater accuracy, (It is a feature of many Rudolf Steiner schools that each class shall spend a few months in a foreign country, usually on an exchange basis with one of the other schools.)

The comprehensiveness of the teaching is seen in Dr. Steiner's recommendation that the proverbs and peculiarities of the particular tongue shall be studied. For instance, the French have a phrase indicating a somewhat sketchy knowledge of their own tongue: *Je parle français comme une vache espagnole.* "I speak French like a Spanish cow." (The derivation is interesting. The proper expression should probably be *un Basque espagnol*—a Spanish Basque, a native of the western end of the Pyrenees, but the transposition of B into V creates a much more imaginative comparison.)

The folklore, nature of the country, the literature and the way of life should also be included, although the time factor sometime hinders this.

Always in the Rudolf Steiner schools, an effort is made to retain the living quality of the language by practising speaking and oral composition.

In the original curriculum, it was recommended that Latin and Greek be introduced at the age of eleven.

However, there is a shortage of teachers with a knowledge of Greek, and there are many children who do not have the mental capacity to be able to cope with Latin in addition to other things, and the teaching of these languages is therefore very much at the discretion of the particular school. That there are advantages in learning them is not in question. Latin grammar provides a very healthy discipline for the mind and a knowledge of these languages obviously contributes much to an understanding of our own.

Etymological studies can be very interesting to children in their teens.There is also the further point that a study of the ancient languages contributes to an understanding of the ancient cultures from which we ourselves have inherited so much. At a suitable age, representative works of the classical authors are studied in the original.

PRACTICAL WORK, HAND AND CRAFTWORK, GARDENING

—Classes One through Five, Handwork, two periods weekly; Classes Six through Eight, Woodwork and Gardening, two hours weekly, interchanging according to season; Classes Nine and Ten, Woodwork and Gardening, two x two-hour weekly periods of each subject, each year; Classes Eleven and Twelve, Bookbinding and Woodwork, two x two-hour weekly periods of each subject, each year.

The Rudolf Steiner school aims at giving children a balanced curriculum. Thus some subjects require the attention of the head forces and some, the hands. Handwork brings children into their limbs and gives them a feeling for what is practical. If we think of the way some people have to walk when thinking or preparing a lecture, we realize how limb activity helps brain activity. This is essentially the case when children learn handwork. Skill and accuracy with the fingers are also assets in practical life.

On coming into Class One, some of the first things told to the children are the reasons why they come to school. Attention is called to the hands and to the fact that with the hands we work.

Objects can be created by the hands and it is an exercise of both the will and the artistic sense to create something original. Initiative is thereby developed. While simple original things can be made in the younger years, e.g., in plasticine, it is with the greater development of skill at about the age of nine that original objects in other media can be produced. There should be a progression to more difficult things in the following years.

Craftwork has a therapeutic value. It is good for the soul. Boys and girls take part in all these activities in the Steiner schools. Boys often show a surprising talent for knitting and sewing, contrary to popular belief, and they take great pleasure in them. Besides the skill there is a social element. Although in adult life certain activities are usually carried out by one sex, it is good that they should be appreciated by the other. Craftwork enhances a sense of achievement.

In making shirts, blouses or any other article of apparel, there is also a social aspect involved. If a boy makes a shirt, he realizes personally what work and skill are involved. When he buys shirts, he will have some appreciation of other people's thought and effort.

Woodcarving means impressing one's will on a piece of recalcitrant matter. Gardening means fostering a relationship with the earth and learning to appreciate the great "mother."

There is a sequence of craft, hand- and practical work which goes through the classes like this:

Class 1	Knitting with two needles
Class 2	Knitting and crochet work
Class 3	Useful articles in either of these media: woollen caps, scarves, jumpers, etc.

Class 4	Exact stitching and embroidery
Class 5	Socks, gloves, dolls, puppets, stuffed animals, individual articles of clothing
Class 6	As Class Five, woodwork, carving simple practical objects, gardening
Class 7	Blouses, shirts onto which could be worked original patterns or designs, woodwork, practical objects, moving toys, gardening
Class 8	Use of the sewing machine, darning, mending, nature of materials, woodwork as in Class Seven, gardening
Class 9	Cane work, basketry, dresses, woodwork, carving, stone sculpture where possible, clay modeling, gardening—practical work where possible, but in any case knowledge of rotations, grafting, etc. Copperwork
Class 10	Embroidered tablecloths using original designs, gardening—knowledge of soils and manures etc., clay modeling, spinning, weaving, Ironwork (forge)
Class 11/12	Bookbinding and leatherwork, cabinetmaking

Most of the suggested activities belong to the particular ages and will be found to meet the pupil's needs and capabilities, but this list is not necessarily comprehensive. A good teacher may find other occupations useful, such as weaving. Gardening is a healthy occupation at all ages.

ART: Painting, Modeling, Drawing, Aesthetics

—Generally throughout the school. In Classes Nine through Twelve, a four-week period.

Art has a particular place in the Steiner schools in that it finds its way into most lessons. Indeed the attempt is made to present all subjects artistically in the first instance, but there are few art lessons, and no art teachers before the upper school.

In the lower classes, water colors and wax crayons are used. In painting, liquid water colors are favored and the first lessons, if they can be called lessons, are directed towards developing a feeling for color in itself. For instance, if blue is placed next to yellow, the effect is different from that of blue placed next to green. The experience of red surrounded by green is different from that of green surrounded by red. An appreciation is fostered for the colors which harmonize, and also for color perspective; for instance, red and yellow approach, whereas blue and purple recede.

Children are encouraged to paint pictures out of the color element itself—not necessarily bearing any resemblance to reality. The colors thus become something real themselves and do not only clothe a form. The use of color in this way also provides a powerful incentive to the child's imagination. A child will happily paint things which would stump the adult, for instance, the seventh day of creation!

Drawing consists of simple forms, symmetrical exercises, gradually leading to free geometrical drawings. At about the age of nine, artistic pictures can be made in diagonal shading technique using colored pencils. In such drawings there are no outlines of things but the form arises through a colored surface of shading. At twelve, the drawing of projections and shadows can be taught, then interpenetrating objects, i.e., a round pole pushed at right angles through a surface produces a circle, but at any other angle an ellipse. Then comes perspective, and at fourteen, artistic appreciation of all that has been learned.

Modeling is another from of artistic activity best started about the age of nine. It helps the power of observation.

Painting, drawing and modeling are used throughout the main lesson period in support of other subjects. Thus painting and drawing in Class One lead to writing. They will be used in the animal and plant periods, in the geography and history lessons. If children illustrate or model something which has a bearing on their work, a sort of digestive process takes place which also activates the will. Painting and modeling, however, should not be copies of objects, but should be, at least in the younger classes, something original produced by the child's imagination.

In the upper school, special periods are set aside for artistic activity. In Class Nine, children have often lost their capacity for painting, and now have lessons in black and white drawing. The contrast is therapeutic and accords with the dual nature of puberty mentioned earlier.

In the following years, painting is practised again, but the adolescents now have to learn how to do consciously what they could do instinctively earlier.

Modeling can be taken a step further and drawing is now connected with mathematics, surveying, or map projections. The upper school needs experts in their subjects.

At the age of fourteen, the intellect is developing, as well as the body. The world is being comprehended by means of thought. Coming into the intellectual age, and puberty, the necessary balance is provided not only by regular artistic activity, but by teaching the history of the various arts. In showing the development of art one is, of course, also showing the development of humanity. These particular lessons are given in periods. Thus in Class Nine, a session of three or four weeks' main lesson is devoted to the history of art. This covers the period from antiquity to Rembrandt. It deals with Egyptian and Greek sculpture and architecture, Renaissance painting up to the expression of personalized humanity in the Dutch masters. Poetry is dealt with in Class Ten, music in Class Eleven, architecture in Class Twelve.

Cultural excursions are organised where possible.

MUSIC

—Singing and recorders several times weekly.
Individual instruments, choir, orchestra.

All classes in a Rudolf Steiner school open with a morning verse appropriate to the age of the pupil. The younger groups affirm the working of the divine in man and nature; the older ones invoke assistance. In the music lesson one might see a counterpart to this. Music can be the means of bringing a spiritual quality into the soul which can then serve other subjects in a metamorphosed way. If one considers just how much children have to sit at their desks listening to verbal expositions—however brilliant and necessary—it is not difficult to imagine that there may also be certain ill effects. The music lesson can displace these.

As music plays such an important part in the Rudolf Steiner education, the attempt is made to develop an understanding and an appreciation for music in every child, even the unmusical, and every child attempts to play some instrument. The experience of music is one which belongs to the wholeness of life and even if children have no great talent for it, they should be present in the lessons.

The activities of the school are: singing, recorder playing, choral singing, instrumental music, with school orchestra for children who have aptitude.

A beginning is made by singing with the young children and letting them learn by using their still-existing faculty of imitation. They progress to the recorder as soon as they can handle it and again learn by imitating what the teacher does. They observe the way in which the fingers move up and down and eventually learn to play simple melodies by ear. This is not easy but can be accomplished with patience at the age of seven or eight. They do not read music or study theory at this age. This progress from singing to playing an instrument also means a development of the will.

In the years from six to nine, teaching is mainly a matter of developing a musical sense by getting the children to listen and to sing or to play simple pieces in unison on the recorder. The experience remains within the melodic sphere, and the pentatonic scale is used in the early classes as far as possible.

Between the ages of ten and twelve, simple theory is studied, for instance, the notes and the scales; this study can be extended in the following years as far as time and space allow. Two-part singing or playing is taken from about the age of eleven, progressing to three- or four-part, and individual instruments other than the recorder can be used.

Between the ages of thirteen and fourteen, musical education has progressed so far that children should be capable of making music because they like it.

In the upper school, the accent is on further instrumental music, choral and solo singing, the further development of musical judgement, study of theory and musical styles.

Children with the necessary talent are grouped into a school orchestra, even if their ages vary. Choral singing is practised in different groups, ages six to ten, eleven to fourteen, fifteen to eighteen, or again those of any age group with real talent can be formed into a school choir. Singing and instrumental music can also be combined into one musical event.

MOVEMENT: Eurythmy and Gymnastics

—One or two lessons of each, weekly.

Eurythmy is an art of movement created by Rudolf Steiner. It is based on the laws of speech and music. It can be called visible speech and visible song because what is expressed in words or music is translated into a movement of the whole body.

To explain the eurythmy syllabus throughout the school presupposes some fair acquaintence with this art and it is, therefore, beyond the scope of the present booklet. However, some indication might be given by considering how each spoken sound has some significance in itself. In *L* there is an unfolding element, in *R,* a rolling motion, in *B,* an enclosing idea. In eurythmy these sounds are expressed by characteristic gestures. Thus when *L* is spoken by the teacher, a gesture illustrative of unfolding is called for. Similarly, *R* rolls. The *B* gesture is one of enclosing. As an illustration of a vowel sound, one could think of *A* (ah) as expressing astonishment, and the gesture would be one of opening-out.

The words of a poem are spoken by the teacher or accompanist and the sounds are translated into movement by the pupils. Thus there arises a visible representation taken from the sound element of the words and not the intellectual content. Similar laws apply to musical interpretations.

While the sounds of a poem or the notes or intervals of a piece of music are being translated into gestures, the pupil or pupils are not merely standing, but move in geometrical forms in accordance with certain choreographic rules. Some of these are very intricate, particularly if large groups are taking part.

As a preliminary, the child in the early classes learns to run in geometrical or graphical forms, learning how to run straight and curved lines, rings, loops and spirals. He learns the different rhythms of poetry—iamb, trochee, dactyl, anapest, by clapping or stepping them. He learns the elementary gestures for the sounds and notes. It is, incidentally, a great training for the sense of hearing.

There are special movements and exercises which are designed to foster a social sense. A special method of marking alliterations develops the will element. There are exercises for developing intelligence or calming an excitable child. Certain exercises can help a child to concentrate. Others can lead an introspective child to appreciate the world around him.

With more conscious control of the limbs and greater comprehension for geometrical pattern, more difficult tasks can be undertaken. By the age of fourteen, pupils should be able to appreciate that different types of poems, e.g., lyric, elegiac, dramatic, comic, require different handling. It is a help in the appreciation of language and literature.

Apart from more difficult work, the object in the upper school is to get the children to penetrate more consciously into what they are doing. Eurythmy has a harmonizing, coordinating effect.

In parenthesis one should perhaps add a few words about eurythmy as an art in its own right. If a performance is being given on a stage, the spectator sees a figure, or a group of figures, moving to the accompaniment of music or poetry. The eurythmists wear simple colored dresses, with floating veils either of contrasting or similar shades, to express the fundamental mood of what is being performed. The lighting also plays an important part, the changing colors with which the stage is suffused following the changing character of the poem or musical composition. Movement, sound and color are blended into one harmonious whole.

It is difficult to write about gymnastics in the Steiner sense. Various indications were given by him but no accepted syllabus was worked out in his lifetime. Several attempts have been made to develop along new lines following his suggestions.

Orthodox gymnastics, or physical culture, suffers from the absence of any soul content. If we are to educate the whole human being, then mind and body must function together. It is not enough to think out exercises which will use this or the other muscle, but we must have exercises in which the whole being of the person takes part. An indication was given that children should imitate the gestures of human work, not necessarily in a realistic way, but rhythmically and figuratively. For instance, one could think of the work of the lumberjacks. The swinging of the axe provides good exercise. Brought into a regular rhythmic movement and then carried out to the accompaniment of a suitable verse spoken by the teacher, both body and mind are occupied in harmony.

One could imagine that a whole lesson could be based on a story with a continuous thread, and into which various exercises could be incorporated.

Such exercises are suitable for children between the ages of nine and twelve. Free play is always possible, with ropes, rope ladders, balls, etc., and children will use their own imagination, which is also good.

From the age of twelve it is obvious that a more precise and strenuous form of gymnastics is necessary, calling for more precision and conscious control. "Orientation in space" is a phrase which one meets in this connection; "experience of the opposing forces of gravity and levity."

The five Greek exercises were: running, jumping, wrestling, discus and javelin throwing. The first two can be practised all through school life; the other three are suitable in the upper school. By "wrestling" is not meant the all-out variety of the professional performers, but where two people stand opposite one another, feet apart and right hands clasped. The object is to bring the opponent out of his position not by mere force, but by dynamic movement.

SPORT

Sport and the facilities for sport will depend on the size of the school and its location. Organised sport is not a fetish in the Rudolf Steiner schools but the opportunity for exercise must be given and it would also be anti-social if games were not included in the curriculum. Thus, team games of various sorts have their place, athletics, tennis, etc. Where possible, there may be after-school groups or clubs for sailing, canoeing, swimming, rock-climbing and so forth.

SURVEYING, TECHNOLOGY, FIRST AID, SHORTHAND, TYPEWRITING

In the original curriculum these things were included. Undoubtedly it is good to learn something of them but sometimes one has to reckon with the limiting time factor.

The first two can be incorporated in the mathematics and science lessons. In the anthropology, physiology, periods it might be possible to touch on first aid. Shorthand has largely been made obsolete by the use of recording and transcribing machines. Typewriting has become Keyboarding and Word-processing and should find a place in the Class Ten/Eleven curriculum. The use of computers should also be taught here.

RELIGION

—Two lessons weekly.

The religion lessons in the Rudolf Steiner school are on a very broad basis. There is nothing in them which is sectarian or dogmatic. In the first Rudolf Steiner school, the ministers of the various denominations came into the school to teach their various groups, but a great many children were not catered for. At the wish of the parents of these children, a general religion lesson was instituted, and this has become a fairly generally accepted pattern although each school makes its own particular arrangements to suit its own circumstances.

Religious feelings and religious impulses are the ones which can move men to do the greatest deeds, be they deeds of devotion or deeds of fanaticism. In the past, all human culture had its roots in religion. Religion is something fundamental to the human being. A mood of religious devotion strengthens the moral fibre.

In religion, thoughts and feelings are lifted above the physical-material world, but insofar as this world is a manifestation of the spiritual, any subject can provide material for a religion lesson. The teacher is free to choose material at will, taking poems, stories, or creating from imagination. The Bible offers obvious material. It should be borne in mind that the giving of factual knowledge is not the aim of the religion lesson, rather is its object the development of a mood of awe, reverence or wonder.

In this particular connection we must take into consideration four stages in child development.

As young children, we are a part of nature, but becoming conscious of an inner world. In our inner world, we feel the mystery of our relationship with a higher power. But the higher power manifests in outer nature as well as in our being. Thus the religious teaching up to the age of nine will strive to explain something of the divine in nature, that everywhere in nature there is spirit. The teacher should also speak of the human being as a manifestation of the divine with the inference that man must strive to be worthy.

Fairy stories or stories characterizing the work of the elemental beings can provide the actual material; also stories of saints or of those in which angels play a part. Plant and animal study with particular reference to the idea of metamorphosis can be valuable, i.e., if one considers the life cycle of a frog, there is the one spiritual entity manifesting itself in various forms. One can speak of sleeping and waking, and the cycle of life and death which shows the working of the spiritual in the physical.

Between the ages of nine and ten, there is an awakening in the child's consciousness. The question arises, "Who am I?" There is a realization of selfhood. As the personality emerges, the time is opportune to speak of Christ and at about age eleven a beginning can be made of a study of the Gospels, beginning with St. Luke. But also at this age, as the mind busies itself with questions of selfhood, it is the time to speak of such matters as destiny, of what belongs to the past and of what to the future. Biographies of people whose lives have perhaps had incisive demands made on them by destiny are useful material, also stories of King Arthur's knights, apart from the Grail series.

At a third stage (eleven, twelve, thirteen, fourteen), comes the question of what is my relationship with other people, and here it is opportune to speak of the immediate effects of the life of Christ and the way His work was carried on by His disciples. The *Acts of the Apostles* are the obvious material, but legends and stories can be used. *Pilgrim's Progress* is an example of good basic material. Let it be repeated that the religion lessons are not primarily informative, but should be designed to develop feelings of a higher nature.

Finally, towards the end of the upper school, the story of the Holy Grail is taken, and a survey is given of the world religions.

Every morning, before the main lesson begins, a verse is spoken by the children appropriate to their age. Although this is not exactly a prayer, it has something of a devotional character. Sometimes, in the upper classes, the Lord's Prayer is added.

As a background to the whole religious teaching, there are the recurring Christian festivals. Christmas is celebrated by all from the youngest children up. Easter is reserved for the upper school. In England Michaelmas almost coincides with the beginning of the new school year, bringing with the passing of outer nature the new awakening forces within humanity. This always seems a fitting festival as teachers and pupils reassemble for a fresh effort.

The object of the religion lessons is to uplift. It is not the purpose of religion in the Rudolf Steiner school to preach or utter well-meaning platitudes or to guide the child to any particular confession. The object is to touch that deeper core of human feeling which slumbers and which when awakened will form a source of moral impulse.

Steiner education originated in a Christian country. As it is now spreading worldwide, adaptations in the curriculum are being made which accord with different cultures.

About the Author

Roy Wilkinson has been connected with the work of Rudolf Steiner for over 60 years. Born in Leicestershire, England, he was educated both locally and in Switzerland. He attended the Goetheanum School of Speech and Drama, receiving his certificate from Frau Dr. Steiner herself.

After working at an educational center, he made excursions into the fields of medicine (with Weleda) and agriculture, and eventually became a teacher. Over some forty years he taught in Steiner and State schools in England, Germany, and Switzerland. He has also taught children in need of special care.

Mr. Wilkinson has been active as an advisor to schools and lecturer on Rudolf Steiner education and Anthroposophy in many European countries, in South America as well as in English-speaking countries.

Another major contribution is the writing he has done over a period of more than twenty years. Wilkinson has produced introductory books on Rudolf Steiner education and its philosophical foundations. These and his curriculum guide booklets have been highly appreciated by teachers, parents, and those seeking answers to personal questions. A complete list of current editions is at the end of this volume.

BOOKS BY ROY WILKINSON

Questions and Answers on Rudolf Steiner Education
The Temperaments in Education
The Interpretation of Fairy Tales
The Curriculum of the Rudolf Steiner School
Commonsense Schooling
Rudolf Steiner on Education

Wilkinson Waldorf Curriculum Series:
Teaching English
Teaching Mathematics
Teaching Physics and Chemistry
Teaching Geography
Teaching History I: *Ancient Civilizations, Greece, Rome*
54£Teaching History II: *Middle Ages, Renaissance to Second World War*
Old Testament Stories
Commentary on the Old Testament Stories
The Norse Stories and Their Significance
Teaching Practical Activities: *Farming, Gardening, Housebuilding*
The Human Being and the Animal World
Plant Study and Geology
Nutrition, Health, and Anthropology
Miscellany: *A Collection of Poems and Plays*
Plays for Puppets

The Origin and Development of Language
The Spiritual Basis of Rudolf Steiner Education

Rudolf Steiner: Aspects of his spiritual world view (3 volumes)
Anthroposophy vol. I: *Rudolf Steiner. Reincarnation and karma. The spiritual nature of the human being. The development of human consciousness.*
Anthroposophy vol. II: *Evolution of the world and humanity. Relationships between the living and the dead. Forces of evil. The modern path of initiation.*
Anthroposophy vol. III: *Life between death and rebirth. The spiritual hierarchies. The philosophical approach to the spirit. The mission of Christ.*

May be ordered from: Rudolf Steiner College Bookstore
9200 Fair Oaks Boulevard
Fair Oaks, CA 95628, USA
Tel: (916) 961-8729 — Fax: (916) 961-3032